THE POWER OF
SEX
TRANSMUTATION

THE POWER OF
SEX
TRANSMUTATION

HOW TO USE THE MOST RADICAL IDEA
FROM *THINK AND GROW RICH*

Mitch Horowitz
Author of *The Miracle Club*

Special Bonus:
Includes Napoleon Hill's Original Chapter,
The Mystery of Sex Transmutation

Published 2019 by Gildan Media LLC
aka G&D Media
www.GandDmedia.com

FIRST EDITION 2019

Front cover design by David Rheinhardt of Pyrographx

Interior design by Meghan Day Healey of Story Horse, LLC

Library of Congress Cataloging-in-Publication Data is available upon
request

ISBN: 978-1-7225-0265-2

10   9   8   7   6   5   4   3   2   1

Contents

Contents

Author's Note

This book is based on a talk I delivered on sex transmutation in the spring of 2019. The response was so enthusiastic—and the questions that followed so spirited—that I decided to adapt the material into this concise book, *The Power of Sex Transmutation*. My hope is that it elucidates one of the most powerful and intriguing yet confounding points in Napoleon Hill's program of success. Following my exploration of this topic you will find an appendix with Hill's original 1937 chapter on sex transmutation from *Think and Grow Rich*. I encourage you to study both carefully and experiment with what you find.

Author's Note

Chapter 1

Why a Book on Sex Transmutation?

This book explores the taboo topic of Napoleon Hill. The use of sexual energy arrives as step ten of thirteen steps to riches in *Think and Grow Rich*. Hill calls it "the mystery of sex transmutation."

Sex transmutation is probably the most intriguing and, in some regards, the most powerful, but also least-understood step in Hill's philosophy of personal achievement. It is also the least discussed. This is because it engenders embarrassment and confusion. You can only imagine how much more so this topic seemed risqué, radical, and even fringe-like in the year 1937 when Napoleon Hill first wrote about it.

Before I get into the specifics of sex transmutation, I want to share a personal revelation that made me realize how taboo a topic this really is. In 1960, more than twenty years after Hill first published *Think and Grow Rich*, one of my heroes, the motivational writer and radio commentator Earl Nightingale recorded a condensed edition of the book. Earl's 1960 condensation omitted the chapter on sex transmutation almost entirely. He neutered it, so to speak, and changed it to "enthusiasm." Gone was any mention of sex transmutation, and in its place was the more benign and somewhat redundant section on the power of enthusiasm. If Earl Nightingale and his publisher were too embarrassed to discuss the topic of sex transmutation in 1960, admittedly a long time ago in a more conservative age, again how much more radical did this subject seem in 1937? And how brave was it of Napoleon Hill to tackle this topic at all?

Now, I was delivering an online seminar on *Think and Grow Rich* shortly before this writing, and I was hitting upon some of the key points of Hill's book. During the question-and-answer session, a participant asked, "Could you please talk about this topic of sex transmutation, because it's completely mysterious to me, it's lost on me, I don't understand it. Can you unpack it?"

I was struck by this question. For these many decades, readers have been reading and rereading

Think and Grow Rich, as well as taking in audio editions, adaptations, commentaries, and online seminars—and still, after generations, the topic of sex transmutation remains mysterious, taboo, intriguing, and often confusing. Here we are in 2019, and a dedicated reader was asking, in effect, "what in the world did he mean by this?"

I was struck by the necessity to treat this topic more fully and openly; because I think it's on everyone's minds, and yet very few commentators on Napoleon Hill have ever really sought to expand on what he means by the "mystery of sex transmutation." That's what we're going to do.

Chapter 2

What Is Sex Transmutation?

Let me begin by explaining exactly what Napoleon Hill meant, because I do believe it can be described in simple terms, even though it is an esoteric subject and probably every explanation—including Hill's own—will bring with it a train of questions, which I will address. But it can be explained plainly, and here it is:

Hill believed, I think with great reason and with great antecedents in a variety of ancient traditions, that the force of life seeking to express itself within us, the force of creativity seeking to express itself in us, is experienced as the *sexual urge*. The sexual urge is what motivates our species to procreate. The sensate experience driving our species toward procreation is experienced as sexual desire. As such, it's extremely powerful, arguably it's overwhelmingly powerful, a topic that we will touch upon later.

It is an urge that brings great joy. It is an urge that brings great suffering. It is an urge that brings people into harmony with one another. It is an urge that brings people into profound conflict. But it is the essential creative urge. It is the life force, so to speak, seeking expression. The sensate experience of sexual satisfaction, of sexual pleasure is how we men and women experience life itself seeking pro-creation, not only on a biological level, *but on all levels.* We are by nature productive beings. We are generative beings. We build things. We solve problems. We create new ones. We create works of art. We maintain commerce. We foster households. We create and tear down buildings, bridges, highways, and structures of all kinds. We devise technologies and seek, with greater and lesser levels of success, to manage the problems and challenges that accompany them. We eradicate old things and put new things, sometimes but not always improved things, in their place.

All of these impulses within the individual, Hill taught, are *the force of life itself seeking expression.* And that force experienced on the most sensate level is the sexual urge. But it is more than simply physical desire or expression—it is the essence of life seeking propagation on all levels and in all ways. Every time you create something, whether financial, artistic, architectural, craft-based, or product-based, this same life force is replicating itself through you.

There is antecedent for Hill's observation in many different traditions: in Taoism, in Kabbalah, in Vedic teachings, and beyond. Sex transmutation is one the deepest aspects of Hill's philosophy. In fact, I think it is the aspect of Hill's philosophy that is most fully connected to other wisdom traditions, and it is the most esoteric.

Now, some seekers today regard Napoleon Hill's works as a kind of spirituality with training wheels. There are people on the path who consider themselves above Napoleon Hill's material, a point of view that I discourage. But among that group of critics there are also those who will concede that he had a very knowing, sophisticated, and practical grasp of the concept of sex energy as it's been expressed in religious traditions and esoteric traditions throughout the ages. They are correct. And here we arrive at the *actionable* part of his teaching.

As noted, Hill saw the sexual urge as the creative impulse seeking expression within men and women, not only biologic expression, but all forms of expression: creative, commercial, and so on. He took this keen observation a step further and said you can actually *harness* and *use* this energy in your life in ways that go beyond the familiar physical releases, and in a manner that adds power to the pursuit of your goals. You do it this way: When you feel a sexual urge, when you feel the wish to express sexual desire, *you as an individual are capable of redirecting that desire towards an expression other than the physical*, towards some other form of expression or creation, and you do this through the mental act of consciously redirecting the sexual urge from physical to creative expression. The creative expression takes the form of whatever your worldly wish is at a given period. This is the act of transmutation. It is, in effect, an act of mental alchemy. You can actually become consciously aware of redirecting or transmuting the urge for sexual expression away from the physical and towards something that you are seeking to create in the world, whether commercial, scholarly, artistic, something physically based, and so forth.

This transmutation adds unique energy, intellect, enthusiasm, resilience, and intuitive insight to whatever you are working on. This is because sexual transmutation consciously places the force of creation itself at the back of your personal efforts.

I must immediately note that Hill is not counseling you to sublimate or repress the sexual urge. Quite the opposite. In the same chapter, Hill also emphasizes that nothing is greater tonic for one's mood, spirit, and physical relaxation and wellness than healthfully expressed, consensual sexuality. He makes that point again and again. This, too, is a very liberated attitude for the year 1937—that physical sexual expression is vital for a sense of wellbeing, and that it probably has greater therapeutic value than anything else we engage in.

So, he's not in any respect talking about sublimation, repression, or abstinence—not at all. But he is making the point that there exist other selective channels through which sexual energy can be expressed, which go beyond the physical. Physical expression is one vital, necessary, helpful means of expression. But there are other creative, commercial, artistic, intellectual, athletic channels through which the sexual impulse can be directed, at the time and place of your choosing.

In fact, Hill notes that greatly effective people in the world, in whatever walk of life—the entrepreneur, the person who excels at a certain art or craft or science, the writer, the actor, the salesman, people who tend to perform at a uniquely high level in their field, and people who tend to be magnetic and enthusiastic and demonstrate the capacity to persuade other people of the soundness of their plans and get other people to go along with them—all of them, often unconsciously, are using sexual energy, and channeling the sexual urge, at critical moments, into their presentation or works. This imbues their works or personalities with greater vigor, substance, and appeal.

Hill makes the observation that, in many cases, such people are of a very highly sexual nature. The sexual urge, he writes, is very heavily pronounced in them, and they are using it all the time, not always knowingly, not always consciously, but they are using it to forward their plans, to rally people to their side, to get things done. Hill specifically uses the example of a salesperson who is exceptionally persuasive—this person's magnetism, he notes, is sexual in nature. But it is a form of transmuted sexuality in which it is not directed toward physicality or intimacy, but rather it is expressed in the manner of charisma or sales appeal. This is why a customer sometimes feels, often mistakenly, that a sales agent is flirting. That may be occurring on some level, but what is more often occurring is the act of sex transmutation—although the practitioner and the subject are unaware of it.

Hill takes matters even further and maintains that people who are commonly regarded as geniuses, as icons, as impresarios are capable of rising to that level of excellence because sexual energy is at the back of their efforts. Again, this energy is the life force itself seeking expression and creation through us in myriad ways. Now, for the plural term geniuses, Hill uses the arcane plural *genii*. This is significant. Genii dates to Roman-Latin usage. It means not only great intellectual prowess but also suggests the Ancient Roman meaning that genius itself is a gift bestowed by higher spirits or daemons. The same term appears as *jinn* or genie in Arab folklore and culture, again referencing a spirit capable of possessing the individual or bestowing supernatural power. This suggests the connection Hill saw between higher forces of life and the individual's capacity for accomplishment.

A similar point was made by the great medical clairvoyant Edgar Cayce (1877–1945), who was roughly contemporaneous with Hill. I have no evidence that the two figures ever met or exchanged ideas. But they reached similar conclusions in this area. In my book, *Occult America*, I write about Cayce advising a young man from Kentucky, a distant cousin who writes to him in the 1930s to say that he is gay, and he doesn't know where to turn, he doesn't know what to do; he's been to different therapists and doctors, and he feels completely at a loss as to how to proceed with his life because all the people around him, given the time and era, pathologize his sexuality.

Cayce, remarkably enough, a man who was raised in the environs of a deeply conservative Bible belt region of the country, replies to this young man with extraordinary sensitivity and insight. Here is a portion of the seer's written response:

> *Sex, of course, is a great factor in everyone's life; it is the line between the great and the vagabond, the good and the bad; it is the expression of reactive forces in our very nature; allowed to run wild, to self-indulgence, becomes physical and mental derangement; turned into the real influence it should be in one's life, connects man closer with his God, and this is the use you should put it to. . . . That your experience has brought you manifestations that have at times, or often, expressed themselves in sex is not to be wondered at, when we realize that that is the expression of creative life on earth.*

I wrote about this episode at the end of Occult America because I wanted to demonstrate what a remarkably sensitive, intuitive, and sympathetic figure Edgar Cayce was that he could write to a young man like that from Kentucky in the 1930s. Edgar's was probably one of the only voices that sounded that way at that time. And, looking back, I think he and Napoleon Hill were in comportment in their attitudes about sexuality. They viewed sexuality as a positive expression, a therapeutic expression, a healthful expression—and something more. Again, Edgar is expressing the view that while the biologic expression of sex is vital and necessary, the sexual urge, in its broadest terms, underscores everything creative that we do. And that's exactly what Hill was driving at.

Chapter 3

Ways of Using
Sex Transmutation

I see two critical steps to employing the power of sex transmutation in your life.

The first is simply to become of aware of it—the concept of sexual energy and its potential transmutation adds a whole new dimension to how we understand human sexuality and creativity. It is certainly not something we're raised to observe. We must see and understand the sexual force in our lives as not only an urge towards physical release and procreation, but as something that is also at the back of our wishes, drives, desires, and efforts.

That awareness places you on more intimate terms with yourself and your nature, which is vitally important because the first step of all productive self-knowledge is knowing thyself. So, that is step one.

In knowing yourself sexually, it is also important to be aware of how this facet of your nature is used to manipulate you. Our consumer society repackages and resells everything, including heroism, rebelliousness, religion, and, of course, sexuality. Every human urge that has its own noble, primal basis in the life of the individual is ultimately repackaged and sold back to us, or potentially used to manipulate us.

Pornography has never been more prevalent in our society because of the digital revolution. I suppose our generation is the first generation that is dealing with the truly mass, 24/7 distribution of pornography. It's existed from time immemorial, of course, going back to Greek vases and Vedic tapestries. Our generation is not unique in this regard, but our generation is unique insofar as this material is being distributed worldwide on demand, and I suppose we have to ask ourselves how this going to affect us. And we don't fully know. I tend to have permissive attitudes towards all these things, but at the same time I do think that we as a species, at least here in the West, are getting somewhat reconditioned sexually because there's such a vast consumption of porngraphy today.

Now, again, I don't know whether that's a wholly good or bad thing, or, as is often the case, there are probably a wide range of consequences spread across a large field of possibilities. It is probable that adolescents, in particular, are getting conditioned along certain lines because of the nature of pornography. I also recognize that there are some people for whom pornography is a positive experience, for whom it alleviates loneliness and sexual urges, and I take that seriously. I also recognize that there are performers doing this for a living, who I believe deserve respect and fair treatment financially. So, there's a complexity of things going on.

Probably the reason we're facing so many challenges in this area, and part of the reason why so much of the traffic that actually goes on within digital culture is sexual in nature, is because Napoleon Hill was correct: the sexual urge is at the back of so much in life. In *Think and Grow Rich*, Napoleon Hill notes that of all the things that seem to urge the individual in a certain direction, that play upon the individual's motivations and desires, and that stimulate the psyche, sexuality is the number-one stimulant. Here is Hill's list of "The Ten Mind Stimuli:"

1. The desire for sex expression

2. Love

3. A burning desire for fame, power, or financial gain, MONEY

4. Music

5. Friendship between either those of the same sex, or those of the opposite sex

6. A Master Mind alliance based upon the harmony of two or more people who ally themselves for spiritual or temporal advancement*

7. Mutual suffering, such as that experienced by people who are persecuted

8. Auto-suggestion

9. Fear

10. Narcotics and alcohol

---

* I write about this in my book *The Power of the Master Mind* (G&D Media).

Obviously, lots of things motivate us. We're motivated by the need for income. We're motivated by peer attitudes. We're motivated by the desire to be appreciated. We're motivated by our fears. As Hill notes, some motivations are substance-based. Our minds and emotions are stimulated, sometimes heightened and sometimes dulled, by various drugs and by alcohol. The wish to know, the wish to attain higher knowledge, is also a form of motivation. Yet amid all of these diffuse motivations, Hill ranks at the top the sexual urge. So, it's natural that marketers and others around us are, in varying ways and either consciously or unconsciously, going to use sexuality to manipulate us. It's inevitable and it requires mindfulness and even wariness. Sometimes the people doing the manipulating are not aware themselves of what is going on.

The power of sex, even in our media-saturated society, is still something of a taboo topic. It still makes people uncomfortable. This is among the reasons why I want to reassure you that everything I am writing about, and the experiments I am about to posit here and in the next chapter, are your own personal, private inquiries. These things belong to the environs of your own psyche. You don't have to run out and share what you're doing. You don't have to seek anyone's approbation or approval. You don't have to identify yourself or adopt some label.

I think our greatest personal experiments are conducted in private, and I invite everyone to explore what I am about to describe knowing that you do not have to take a communal or congregational approach to any of this. These sexual explorations are yours alone, and I think that sense of privacy, that sense of silence, invites you to study, consider, experiment, to get to know yourself in a different way.

Now, the second step takes us further into the question of application. To review, Hill makes the contention, and I believe this is true from my own personal experience, that when you are possessed of the sexual urge, you can—by a shift in your attention—redirect that urge from physical satisfaction toward the accomplishment of another aim, whether commercial, artistic, educative, or creative. Remember: you're not repressing physical satisfaction. Rather, you are electing to make a choice in a self-selected situation. This act will place greater and deeper vigor, insight, and energy behind your efforts.

You may be writing a chapter in a book. You may be delivering a sales presentation. You may be building a home. You may be practicing a dance routine or a martial arts combination. Whatever you're dedicated to, you can do consciously what we're doing unconsciously all the time by harnessing sexual energy as a creative force, as a creative impetus. It's going on constantly whether we're directing it or not.

In life we're sitting in the passenger seat most of the time. But through a shift in our attention we can, at a choice moment, transmute these creative, sexual energies. Again, we already do it unconsciously; when people are filled with excitement and enthusiasm and a positive, fearless, can-do attitude; when they are passionately applying themselves in the direction of a natural and cherished task—there is sexual energy present.

People are always telling me things like, "You're so enthusiastic." "You seem never to sleep"—I do sleep, by the way. And, "you produce so much in terms of books and lectures and shows and narration. How do you do it?" I say, "It's love for the subject matter. I'm deeply impassioned towards my subjects. I'm very driven to do it." Napoleon Hill would say, in effect, "Yes, bravo to that—that's true; but there's sex energy at the back of all the terms you're using. You're using euphemisms."

He would probably make the point that passion itself is a euphemism. Magnetism is a euphemism. Even enthusiasm, that elixir that seems to make everything possible, is a euphemism. He would say behind all of that is the sexual urge which is the urge of life seeking creation, generativity, and productivity.

Now, we have to allow ourselves to relax about all of this. There are not always times where sexual redirection is possible. Sometimes sexual expression, of whatever form, requires engagement and release. That's just human nature. So, I don't want people to get hung up over this. I'm not trying to create another rule under which you feel driven to live. Sexuality doesn't obey rules, in any case. But there are select times where you will find, if you experiment, that you *can* redirect the sexual urge in a healthful, natural way along different lines, specifically creative lines.

There are also ways in which this occurs more subtly. One of the things that Napoleon Hill writes about—and here I'm a little hamstrung by some of the old-fashioned language and gender roles that Hill used back in 1937, but the point retains its substance—is that one of the greatest drives behind the creative process, in his language, is man's wish to please woman. Hill writes this in *Think and Grow Rich*, and here I use the original language:

> *Man's greatest motivating force is his desire to please woman! The hunter who excelled during prehistoric days, before the dawn of civilization, did so, because of his desire to appear great in the eyes of woman. Man's nature has not changed in this respect. The "hunter" of today brings home no skins of wild animals, but he indicates his desire for her favor by supplying fine clothes, motor cars, and wealth. Man has the same desire to please woman that he had before the dawn of civilization. The only thing that has changed, is his method of pleasing. Men who accumulate large fortunes, and attain to great heights of power and fame, do so, mainly, to satisfy their desire to please women.*

This same point is captured, albeit in a grim and haunting way, in the movie *The Social Network*, written by Aaron Sorkin. *The Social Network* is about the rise of Facebook as a new technology and media titan. In the movie, these young programmers are feverishly trying to assemble Facebook, particularly Mark Zuckerberg, who appears as a conflicted, socially awkward wizard. He and his generally male collaborators and competitors are in, in essence, trying to "hook up" by presenting themselves as successful, entrepreneurial, hard-driven models of achievement and money.

If you watch the film, which I highly recommend, you'll see the undercurrent of sexuality running through all two hours. It's a vexing and curious aspect of human nature, but what they were expressing in that film, in a somewhat critical way, was what Napoleon Hill was expressing in a more holistic way. He was saying that the nexus of sex and success is simply a fact of human nature. Great people throughout the ages, and in our own time, have often been driven to heights of success because of their desire to please or attract a mate.

In a more idealistic way, a friend of mine who is a champion bicyclist was told by a groomsman at his wedding: "Dude, you were nowhere without her." That, too, implies what Hill was driving at. Hill maintains that in a subtle but extremely powerful way the energy of the individual is very often directed and focused both by his or her mate and by the desire to please that mate.

Now, you'll notice I'm using gender-neutral language at this point, and for a reason. Hill's generation didn't use gender-neutral language; he wrote in the days where people would use expressions, like "behind every great man, there's a woman." It's no aspersion to say that he wrote in gender roles of an earlier generation. To address that, for any who are put off by it, I have also created a gender-neutral edition of *Think and Grow Rich*, and in that gender-neutral edition I preserve all of Hill's arguments faithfully but I break us out of some of the gender stereotypes a bit. If you like what I'm describing, you can go to the sexuality chapter of the gender-neutral edition of *Think and Grow Rich*, and you can take it in without feeling that you have to buy into the sexual roles that belong to an earlier generation.

My point is that whenever Hill talks about man's desire to please woman, we can talk about an individual's desire to please his or her mate or prospective mate. He says that there's a lot of people in our world and in history who have performed extraordinary services, demonstrated things never thought possible, produced endur- ing works of art, feats of entrepreneurship, acts of commerce that have changed the world, who were driven by this very intimate, sexualized wish to please a mate.

It's also important to note that Hill wanted people to express sexual energy in all of its facets, but never in ways there were destructive. That means expressing it in a manner that is obviously consensual, that is respectful, and that is, ultimately if not always, based in love or intimacy. It's interesting, I got into this discussion on an online seminar about *Think and Grow Rich* where somebody asked about the negative dimensions of sex energy. We live in a world today where we're seeing lots of lives that have been torn apart by the misuses of sexual energy. It strikes people as very curious sometimes.

Around the time of my seminar, I was at a dinner party where a very successful entrepreneur was sitting at the head of the table, and he was remarking that we live in a world today where some extreme high-achievers have gotten caught up in sexual scandals or acts of non-consensual behavior, and they seem to have put their whole lives and careers on the line, and hurt others, and it just seems to be a wild lapse of judgment. What's it all about? he wondered. I thought about some of what Napoleon Hill wrote. He talks about the dangers of sexual energy running amok; sexuality, he noted, is so powerful, and it's so irresistible a force when people aren't developed in some other way, that this force of ultimate creation becomes a force of ultimate destruction.

It's almost a part of natural law or human nature that what can nurture can also damage. Light concentrated can heat and heal, but can also cut like a laser. Water can sustain terrestrial life or in excess suffocate it. These are natural laws, and they're also psychological and physical laws. Hill warned that if misused, misdirected, or uncontrolled, the creative urge becomes a destructive urge, and I think that helps decipher some of what's gone on in our culture.

Now, for those of you who are interested in esoteric practices, it's entirely natural to ponder the connection between Hill's observation and the contemporary practice of what is called sex magick. He doesn't talk specifically about that connection, but I do think that what he's talking about relates to sex magick. Simply put, sex magick is setting an intention at the point of climax. I'm simplifying it, because there is often ceremony and ritual involved, but in various ways, sex magick is setting a personal intention or wish at the point of climax or orgasm.

A lot of what we call ceremonial magick, chaos magick, or spell work is actually New Thought along other ritual lines or channels. The basic premise behind modern magick is that the will can be externalized, and that the mental picture or wish can be concretized and actualized in the world around us, through rites, focus, and ceremony. Now, for those of us who are dedicated to New Thought, that practice generally involves externalizing thought through emotionalized focus, affirmations, visualizations, prayers, and mental imagery. But there are many people who I love, respect, and work with who are engaged in witchcraft, spell work, chaos magick, ceremonial magick, and other modalities, who are, to a very great extent, trying to accomplish the same thing—to render thoughts causative—through other means. They might be using herbs, ceremony, deity worship, rituals, symbols, sigils—but we're all attempting the same thing, which is to externalize the images and wishes of the psyche.

The method to which I've been referring has existed in magical tradition for many generations, but was popularized in the modern world by the artist and magician Aleister Crowley, among a handful of others, including the occultist Paschal Beverly Randolph. Their work occurred in the late nineteenth and early twentieth centuries and formed the basis for a lot of ceremonial magick today.

Sex magick as alluded, often involves focusing on a desire, focusing intentions, at the moment of climax. This practice is also used in a somewhat different way in chaos magick as part of the ceremony called sigil magick. In using sigil magick, you formulate a passionate desire—one that has some worldly means of realization—and, through a variety of methods, many of them very simple, render that desire into a symbol, an abstract symbol of the thing wished for. You then "charge" that symbol, so to speak, by working yourself up into a state of ecstasy or some kind of a meditative state that crosses over into a transcendental, surreal, or extra-rational state. Most often this is done through sexual climax.

The creation of the sigil is accomplished by writing down a simple statement of your desire, crossing out select letters, and then rearranging the remaining letters into an abstract symbol. There are myriad methods of doing this—you can create your own. And the key operation is then, during sexual climax, whether it's climax with a partner or whether it's solitary climax, focusing on your desire over the symbol or sigil and thus charging it. Although there are other methods, people generally use orgasm to charge the sigil with sexual-psychical energy. After this, you are effectively supposed to forget all about your desire, insofar as the ceremony itself has fulfilled it. Once charged, the abstract symbol, so the theory goes, becomes a subconscious router of your desire, and results in its fulfillment or outpicturing in the world. There is a gray area, or area of debate, as to how precisely this occurs. This is, after all, an occult practice—though some practitioners argue for its sheer rationality based on its success rate. If you want to learn about the practice, the finest book I personally know of is *Advanced Magick for Beginners* by Alan Chapman. Chapman's book is a marvel of clarity and wit.

Personally speaking, I have not had results with sigil magick—but lots of people I respect have. I think the hang up for me is the notion of "forgetting" one's desire. I am so impassioned toward my desires, and so driven toward them, that I cannot enter the proper psychical state of feeling fulfillment through alternate means, unless they are veritably equal to the thing sought. The ceremonial act in sigil magick is supposed to create a sense of satisfaction, but for me personally it has not. You may be different. Again, lots of people find success using the method. I encourage trying it. But what I've described in my experience is why I personally favor Hill's method of sexual transmutation, which channels sexual energy toward the actual production of the end being sought.

Hill doesn't specifically talk about any these operations I've been describing, such as sex magick or sigil magick. Their popularity came much later. I cannot say for sure what he knew or didn't know about this magical subculture or its methods. But the important thing, for me, is identifying those areas where earnest seekers reach parallel conclusions, even, or especially, if they are not directly in contact. Correspondences are, to me, a marker of truth. I think that what Hill explores affirms all of these operations. Because Hill is really saying that mental and sexual energy possess an extra-physical component, a non-local component. I am absolutely certain, from years of reading and studying and working with Hill's ideas, that he would have agreed that sexual energy, as with the emotions, as with the intellect, has an extra-physical component. He implies as much by identifying sexuality as the incipient life force in the individual.

In fact, in his chapter on sex transmutation he notes that the practice contributes to the development of a "sixth sense," or what we might call extra-sensitivity, ESP, telepathy, or heightened intuition. He did believe that channeled sexual energy could not only amp up your creative, physical, and intellectual abilities, but it would similarly amp up your intuitive abilities to the point where an individual could participate in a kind of "over-mind" or non-localized intelligence or Infinite Intelligence, as he called it. Indeed, Hill wrote that genius itself—again harkening to the Ancient Roman tradition—reaches us through the agencies of a sixth sense. This idea also appeared in the late-ancient Greek-Egyptian philosophy called Hermeticism, which is probably where the Romans received it.

For these reasons, I feel certain that Hill would have agreed that sex energy has an extra-physical component. It exists in the cosmos as an energetic reality and it is expressed through the individual. So, I think this is at the back of the operations performed by today's sex magicians or chaos magicians or people working with sigil magick. As I alluded earlier, the idea of sexually charging your sigil or symbol can seem very abstract. I'm using figurative language to describe operations whose workings we don't really understand. But there is empiricism present. And that empiricism is experienced in the congruency of the results. We certainly have reliable testimony, records of experiences, and successes, but, for all that, we don't really understand what's going on. Things that exist beyond the operation of the five senses can be very difficult to theorize over. In that sense, we don't yet possess a theory of delivery of sex magick. We don't know precisely what's happening. It's extra-physical. It's extrasensory. But I think Hill would affirm by observation, by testimony, by experience that's what's happening is actual, that it's real.

I think people who engage in those forms of magick would benefit from reading Hill's chapter, because it's a very simple and harmonious parallel path. It's interesting, to this day, you mention the name Aleister Crowley, and some people cringe and say, "Oh wow, the Great Beast." He has this outlaw image, which he cultivated. But you mention the name Napoleon Hill, and it seems very domestic. You think of guys sitting around a business roundtable, and it seems very familiar and tame by comparison. And yet, what Hill wrote about sex transmutation is every bit as radical, as daring, and experimental as what Crowley wrote on sex magick. And I personally find Hill's approach easer for the individual to enter into.

Now, I mentioned earlier that Hill's ideas also coalesce with ancient esoteric teachings on sexuality, including those found in Taoism and Tantra, where sexual energy is seen as an actual force that can be cultivated, stored, and used for purposes of transmutation or personal alchemy, by which I mean self-transformation. Now, remarkably enough, here's Napoleon Hill in 1937 in what, comparatively speaking, was a conformist, somewhat repressed society, dealing with some of this deeply esoteric material, sometimes echoing age-old esoteric traditions. It should bring us a new dimension of respect towards Napoleon Hill. When this man says he spent twenty years researching *Think and Grow Rich*, that should be taken very seriously because he looked in a lot of corners and byways and devised a truly remarkable, wide-ranging program, which I'm focusing on just one aspect of here.

But, for me, this focus feels like a kind of breakthrough because, for all the popularity of motivational and inspirational methods in our culture, this topic is rarely dealt with, and you and I have just broken that barrier.

Almost everyone would agree that the energy that we experience at the point of climax feels extraordinary. People cross oceans for it. Every sensitive reader of *Think and Grow Rich* for the past several decades has encountered this teaching on sex transmutation and has said to him or herself, "I know this is vital; I know this is powerful; I know this is important; but I don't know precisely what's going on here." There aren't a lot of places in our culture where you can have that exchange. So, I'm so glad we're having it. My hope is that this discussion becomes a true resource for people.

Chapter 4

Sex Energy in Ancient Cultures— and Our Own

A few months prior to this writing I travelled to Egypt with my friend Ronni Thomas, a brilliant filmmaker. Ronni and I are collaborating on a documentary about the occult book, *The Kybalion*. Although it's a modern book, written in 1908, *The Kybalion* does retain some ideas from the late-ancient Greek-Egyptian philosophy called Hermeticism, which I mentioned earlier. The author of that book was a thoughtful and dynamic New Thought writer named William Walker Atkinson (1862–1932), who wrote under the pseudonym Three Initiates. In *The Kybalion*, Atkinson writes about the principle of "mental gender," that is, about the male or conscious mind impregnating the female or subliminal mind with an idea, which the subliminal or subconscious mind allows to gestate and finally come to life in the world. In Egypt there are bas-reliefs and statues everywhere that are tributes to sexuality and fertility, both of the literal and metaphysical type. There are gods and goddesses specifically dedicated to beauty, to procreation, to fertility—and as the great Hermetic dictum goes, "as above, so below." In other worlds, all facets of the cosmos, nature, and our psyches reflect these energies of sexuality and impregnation, sometimes physically and sometimes metaphysically, not dissimilar from what Atkinson and Hill are writing about.

I was personally able to enter a chamber deep within the Valley of Kings in Luxor, which is normally closed off to the public. I was permitted to go deeply into this chamber and I was permitted to touch the bas-relief of a bull, which is associated in Ancient Egypt with both fertility and sexuality. I can only report back to you what I personally experienced: as I laid hands very gently on this bas-relief of a bull, this symbol of sexual energy and fertility, I felt a sense of absolute lightening go through my body. What was occurring? What was the actual process? I don't know, but I can testify that's what I experienced. The Egyptians clearly recognized the act of creation, the act of sexuality, as something that is as essential as life and death, or the passing to the other world; it was a foundational part of the existential psychology of Ancient Egypt, and it was enshrined within their pantheon.

There's an important point I want to make about personal appearance. You can heighten your magnetic power through your manner of dress, style, and personal comportment. Hill believed, and I've certainly seconded this in my writings, that there's a powerful and important psychology behind clothing and choice of appearance. He believed it necessary to dress in a personally comfortable and self-affirming way, or to adopt whatever kind of gait or composure you wish—and that the right decision in this area would make you feel magnetic, charismatic, confident. And you will actually *be* these things. We underestimate the interplay of the inner and the outer. Both are part of the same whole.

Hence, outer appearance can maximize sexual energy. When we're designing how we dress, wear our hair, the accouterments we wear, when we're designing our image—not just dressing up but designing our image, whatever our definition of that may be—we are seeking to exalt, build, and maximize our sexual energy, in the broadest sense. We're seeking to magnify that creative force, that force of attraction, within ourselves. I think that one should not underestimate or wave off as vanity the importance of dressing and comporting yourself the way that you wish.

I don't make a division between the inner and the outer. I think all of these divisions are artificial past a certain point. No one should feel embarrassed, or be made to feel like they're being shallow, if and when they wish to pay attention to the outer, to appearances, to what makes them look good, to what makes them feel good according to whatever one's internal lights may be, and in whichever way they're directed. It's a self-driven decision.

Of course, we all experience social pressure, peer pressure, consumer pressure; but bear in mind that every society in history—the Hebrews, the Greeks, the Maya, the ancient Vedic culture—every society in its works of art and communication has depicted beauty. We're not the first. And yes there's peer pressure, yes there's consumerism, there's pressure to conform, but every society has had its adornments and its symbols of beauty and its depictions of sexuality from the Song of Solomon to the headdresses of the Native Americans. Every society has had a love for and appreciation of beauty, as they conceived it.

I just want the individual to feel as comfortable and at home in his or her own skin as possible, and I want the individual to feel the approbation to comport, dress, and conduct themselves in the world as comfortably as they personally wish. It's very powerful and its very relaxing. I believe that this is one of the reasons why a transgender person who is transitioning will often describe feeling a great and wonderful sense of relief because they finally feel like they're carrying themselves in the world as they wish, and that's vitally important.

I have two sons and I've been asked how, or whether, to teach kids about this material. I often tell people that when it comes to childrearing I'm reminded of something that was attributed to Napoleon. I don't know if he actually said it. So many things are attributed to Napoleon, apocryphally or not. But it's this: "Every plan immediately fails upon contact with the enemy." Forgive the metaphor, but that's been my experience with childrearing. Every well-laid plan that I seek to enact with my kids seems to completely fall apart in the to-and-fro of actual life; and yet at the same time, they do learn from me; they learn from example, both good and bad. They learn from what they witness in my behavior, strong and weak. And so I'll realize they are listening. They're just not listening at the times when I think they are.

So, it's a very personal question how everybody deals with this. It depends upon the nature of your household, the language you use, the necessity you feel in the matter, and, of course, their age. I've often thought that there should be a *Think and Grow Rich* for young people. I've often thought about writing such a book, and maybe these questions will reignite that in me. Perhaps I'll write such a book that can be handed to a sensitive 13-year-old and will include a chapter that's age-appropriate that deals with some of this material. That might be one response.

I want to reinforce that every being, every mature sexual being, is absolutely using his or her sexual energy in varied ways—the question is will we use it constructively, and how broad a definition are we willing to sustain of that? We understand something about what it means to encourage teens to be responsible from a sexual perspective, but if we broaden our perspective on sexuality, which is really what this book is about, then how much more so can we talk about the responsible and powerful uses of it for all of us? It's a daunting and promising prospect.

I don't want you to feel discouraged if some of this still seems far out or difficult to grasp. We are dealing with esoteric material, not only in the work of Napoleon Hill, but in many religious traditions across the ages. These were things that were matters of deep esotericism to Vedic masters to Taoist masters to Kabbalistic masters. I've tried to distill matters down in as clear a fashion as possible, but to a certain degree, there are places where you must go by yourself. And garnering experience is ultimately a solitary journey. You have to go into this journey yourself. Go into it privately. Glean your own insights. Arrive at your own testimony, at your own experiences.

I say that this material is esoteric because we're trying to find a way of channeling and directing some of the most mysterious forces in human life. The most important thing is that we *try* because that presents payoffs in your own life and encourages the work of other people. Your practice presents guideposts and testimony for others. If you read the book and you say, "I still don't know what he's talking about," you're not wrong—the completion comes with the effort. Try, try. This is mysterious material, and you shouldn't feel frustrated if it doesn't disclose itself all at once.

I want to close with a guided meditation. Depending on what form you're experiencing this book, you can have someone read this passage to you, you can record it, or you can listen back to my narration at your own pace. Prepare by just relaxing and sitting or laying down comfortably. Close your eyes. Take a few deep breaths.

I'd like you to think of something that you deeply wish to achieve in life. Something that is profoundly and powerfully important to you. It can be a certain attainment, a personal achievement, an artistic or career goal. Something that is cherished by you as an aim, as a goal, as a wish.

Once you have a clear picture of the desired or cherished thing, I want you to understand that there is, at the back of this desire, a great, eternal, universal force of self-expression seeking to actualize itself through you. There is a great force of creation seeking to express itself in your experience. This force goes under many names: enthusiasm, creativity, generativity.

But it is ultimately the force of creation itself. It is sexual energy seeking expression and actualization. It is the sexual force that seeks to propagate our species, and this same all-powerful sexual force seeks expression not only as a biologic fact, but as a fact in all areas of creativity, productivity, generativity, and self-expression.

I want you to feel heartened and enthused by the truth that this eternal, universal force exists at the back of your deepest desires and wishes. Because those same desires and wishes are life itself seeking expression through you.

I want you to become aware of yourself as a conscious, creative being who, in your own person, is an individualized agent of this vast universal force of creation. This force is seeking an outlet right now through you and through the medium of your productive desires. Allow yourself to become aware of that.

Take a few more deep breaths in this awareness. Now, in a few moments, I invite you to open your eyes.

You are that.

About the Author

Mitch Horowitz is a PEN Award-winning historian and the author of books including *Occult America; One Simple Idea: How Positive Thinking Reshaped Modern Life;* and *The Miracle Club: How Thoughts Become Reality.* A lecturer-in-residence at the Philosophical Research Society in Los Angeles, Mitch introduces and edits G&D Media's line of Condensed Classics and is the author of the Napoleon Hill Success Course series, including *The Miracle of a Definite Chief Aim, The Power of the Master Mind,* and *Secrets of Self-Mastery.* Visit him at MitchHorowitz.com.

The Mystery of Sex Transmutation

By Napoleon Hill

The meaning of the word "transmute" is, in simple language, "the changing, or transferring of one element, or form of energy, into another."

The emotion of sex brings into being a state of mind.

Because of ignorance on the subject, this state of mind is generally associated with the physical, and because of improper influences, to which most people have been subjected, in acquiring knowledge of sex, things essentially physical have highly biased the mind.

The emotion of sex has back of it the possibility of three constructive potentialities, they are:

1. The perpetuation of mankind.

2. The maintenance of health, (as a therapeutic agency, it has no equal).

3. The transformation of mediocrity into genius through transmutation.

Sex transmutation is simple and easily explained. It means the switching of the mind from thoughts of physical expression, to thoughts of some other nature.

Sex desire is the most powerful of human desires. When driven by this desire, men develop keenness of imagination, courage, will-power, persistence, and creative ability unknown to them at other times. So strong and impelling is the desire for sexual contact that men freely run the risk of life and reputation to indulge it. When harnessed, and redirected along other lines, this motivating force maintains all of its attributes of keenness of imagination, courage, etc., which may be used as powerful creative forces in literature, art, or in any other profession or calling, including, of course, the accumulation of riches.

The transmutation of sex energy calls for the exercise of will-power, to be sure, but the reward is worth the effort. The desire for sexual expression is inborn and natural. The desire cannot, and should not be submerged or eliminated. But it should be given an outlet through forms of expression which enrich the body, mind, and spirit of man. If not given this form of outlet, through transmutation, it will seek outlets through purely physical channels.

A river may be dammed, and its water controlled for a time, but eventually, it will force an outlet. The same is true of the emotion of sex. It may be submerged and controlled for a time, but its very nature causes it to be ever seeking means of expression. If it is not transmuted into some creative effort it will find a less worthy outlet.

Fortunate, indeed, is the person who has discovered how to give sex emotion an outlet through some form of creative effort, for he has, by that discovery, lifted himself to the status of a genius.

Scientific research has disclosed these significant facts:

1. The men of greatest achievement are men with highly developed sex natures; men who have learned the art of sex transmutation.

2. The men who have accumulated great fortunes and achieved outstanding recognition in literature, art, industry, architecture, and the professions, were motivated by the influence of a woman.

The research from which these astounding discoveries were made, went back through the pages of biography and history for more than two thousand years. Wherever there was evidence available in connection with the lives of men and women of great achievement, it indicated most convincingly that they possessed highly developed sex natures.

The emotion of sex is an "irresistible force," against which there can be no such opposition as an "immovable body." When driven by this emotion, men become gifted with a super power for action. Understand this truth, and you will catch the significance of the statement that sex transmutation will lift one to the status of a genius.

The emotion of sex contains the secret of creative ability.

Destroy the sex glands, whether in man or beast, and you have removed the major source of action. For proof of this, observe what happens to any animal after it has been castrated. A bull becomes as docile as a cow after it has been altered sexually. Sex alteration takes out of the male, whether man or beast, all the FIGHT that was in him. Sex alteration of the female has the same effect.

THE TEN MIND STIMULI

The human mind responds to stimuli, through which it may be "keyed up" to high rates of vibration, known as enthusiasm, creative imagination, intense desire, etc. The stimuli to which the mind responds most freely are:—

1. The desire for sex expression

2. Love

3. A burning desire for fame, power, or financial gain, MONEY

4. Music

5. Friendship between either those of the same sex, or those of the opposite sex.

6. A Master Mind alliance based upon the harmony of two or more people who ally themselves for spiritual or temporal advancement.

7. Mutual suffering, such as that experienced by people who are persecuted.

8. Auto-suggestion

9. Fear

10. Narcotics and alcohol.

The desire for sex expression comes at the head of the list of stimuli, which most effectively "step-up" the vibrations of the mind and start the "wheels" of physical action. Eight of these stimuli are natural and constructive. Two are destructive. The list is here presented for the purpose of enabling you to make a comparative study of the major sources of mind stimulation. From this study, it will be readily seen that the emotion of sex is, by great odds, the most intense and powerful of all mind stimuli.

This comparison is necessary as a foundation for proof of the statement that transmutation of sex energy may lift one to the status of a genius. Let us find out what constitutes a genius.

Some wiseacre has said that a genius is a man who "wears long hair, eats queer food, lives alone, and serves as a target for the joke makers." A better definition of a genius is, "a man who has discovered how to increase the vibrations of thought to the point where he can freely communicate with sources of knowledge not available through the ordinary rate of vibration of thought."

The person who thinks will want to ask some questions concerning this definition of genius. The first question will be, "How may one communicate with sources of knowledge which are not available through the ORDINARY rate of vibration of thought?"

The next question will be, "Are there known sources of knowledge which are available only to genii, and if so, WHAT ARE THESE SOURCES, and exactly how may they be reached?"

We shall offer proof of the soundness of some of the more important statements made in this book— or at least we shall offer evidence through which you may secure your own proof through experimentation, and in doing so, we shall answer both of these questions.

"GENIUS" IS DEVELOPED
THROUGH THE SIXTH SENSE

The reality of a "sixth sense" has been fairly well established. This sixth sense is "Creative Imagination." The faculty of creative imagination is one which the majority of people never use during an entire lifetime, and if used at all, it usually happens by mere accident. A relatively small number of people use, WITH DELIBERATION AND PURPOSE AFORETHOUGHT, the faculty of creative imagination. Those who use this faculty voluntarily, and with understanding of its functions, are GENII.

The faculty of creative imagination is the direct link between the finite mind of man and Infinite Intelligence. All so-called revelations, referred to in the realm of religion, and all discoveries of basic or new principles in the field of invention, take place through the faculty of creative imagination.

When ideas or concepts flash into one's mind, through what is popularly called a "hunch," they come from one or more of the following sources:—

1. Infinite Intelligence

2. One's subconscious mind, wherein is stored every sense impression and thought impulse which ever reached the brain through any of the five senses

3. From the mind of some other person who has just released the thought, or picture of the idea or concept, through conscious thought, or

4. From the other person's subconscious storehouse.

There are no other KNOWN sources from which "inspired" ideas or "hunches" may be received.

The creative imagination functions best when the mind is vibrating (due to some form of mind stimulation) at an exceedingly high rate. That is, when the mind is functioning at a rate of vibration higher than that of ordinary, normal thought.

When brain action has been stimulated, through one or more of the ten mind stimulants, it has the effect of lifting the individual far above the horizon of ordinary thought, and permits him to envision distance, scope, and quality of THOUGHTS not available on the lower plane, such as that occupied while one is engaged in the solution of the problems of business and professional routine.

When lifted to this higher level of thought, through any form of mind stimulation, an individual occupies, relatively, the same position as one who has ascended in an airplane to a height from which he may see over and beyond the horizon line which limits his vision, while on the ground. Moreover, while on this higher level of thought, the individual is not hampered or bound by any of the stimuli which circumscribe and limit his vision while wrestling with the problems of gaining the three basic necessities of food, clothing, and shelter. He is in a world of thought in which the ORDINARY, work-a-day thoughts have been as effectively removed as are the hills and valleys and other limitations of physical vision, when he rises in an airplane.

While on this exalted plane of THOUGHT, the creative faculty of the mind is given freedom for action. The way has been cleared for the sixth sense to function, it becomes receptive to ideas which could not reach the individual under any other circumstances. The "sixth sense" is the faculty which marks the difference between a genius and an ordinary individual.

The creative faculty becomes more alert and receptive to vibrations, originating outside the individual's subconscious mind, the more this faculty is used, and the more the individual relies upon it, and makes demands upon it for thought impulses. This faculty can be cultivated and developed only through use.

That which is known as one's "conscience" operates entirely through the faculty of the sixth sense.

The great artists, writers, musicians, and poets become great, because they acquire the habit of relying upon the "still small voice" which speaks from within, through the faculty of creative imagination. It is a fact well known to people who have "keen" imaginations that their best ideas come through so-called "hunches."

There is a great orator who does not attain to greatness, until he closes his eyes and begins to rely entirely upon the faculty of Creative Imagination. When asked why he closed his eyes just before the climaxes of his oratory, he replied, "I do it, because, then I speak through ideas which come to me from within."

One of America's most successful and best known financiers followed the habit of closing his eyes for two or three minutes before making a decision. When asked why he did this, he replied, "With my eyes closed, I am able to draw upon a source of superior intelligence."

The late Dr. Elmer R. Gates, of Chevy Chase, Maryland, created more than 200 useful patents, many of them basic, through the process of cultivating and using the creative faculty. His method is both significant and interesting to one interested in attaining to the status of genius, in which category Dr. Gates, unquestionably belonged. Dr. Gates was one of the really great, though less publicized scientists of the world.

In his laboratory, he had what he called his "personal communication room." It was practically sound proof, and so arranged that all light could be shut out. It was equipped with a small table, on which he kept a pad of writing paper. In front of the table, on the wall, was an electric pushbutton, which controlled the lights. When Dr. Gates desired to draw upon the forces available to him through his Creative Imagination, he would go into this room, seat himself at the table, shut off the lights, and CONCENTRATE upon the KNOWN factors of the invention on which he was working, remaining in that position until ideas began to "flash" into his mind in connection with the UNKNOWN factors of the invention.

On one occasion, ideas came through so fast that he was forced to write for almost three hours. When the thoughts stopped flowing, and he examined his notes, he found they contained a minute description of principles which had not a parallel among the known data of the scientific world. Moreover, the answer to his problem was intelligently presented in those notes. In this manner Dr. Gates completed over 200 patents, which had been begun, but not completed, by "half-baked" brains. Evidence of the truth of this statement is in the United States Patent Office.

Dr. Gates earned his living by "sitting for ideas" for individuals and corporations. Some of the largest corporations in America paid him substantial fees, by the hour, for "sitting for ideas."

The reasoning faculty is often faulty, because it is largely guided by one's accumulated experience. Not all knowledge, which one accumulates through "experience," is accurate. Ideas received through the creative faculty are much more reliable, for the reason that they come from sources more reliable than any which are available to the reasoning faculty of the mind.

The major difference between the genius and the ordinary "crank" inventor, may be found in the fact that the genius works through his faculty of creative imagination, while the "crank" knows nothing of this faculty. The scientific inventor (such as Mr. Edison, and Dr. Gates), makes use of both the synthetic and the creative faculties of imagination.

For example, the scientific inventor, or "genius," begins an invention by organizing and combining the known ideas, or principles accumulated through experience, through the synthetic faculty (the reasoning faculty). If he finds this accumulated knowledge to be insufficient for the completion of his invention, he then draws upon the sources of knowledge available to him through his *creative* faculty. The method by which he does this varies with the individual, but this is the sum and substance of his procedure:

1. HE STIMULATES HIS MIND SO THAT IT VIBRATES ON A HIGHER-THAN-AVERAGE PLANE, using one or more of the ten mind stimulants or some other stimulant of his choice.

2. HE CONCENTRATES upon the known factors (the finished part) of his invention, and creates in his mind a perfect picture of unknown factors (the unfinished part), of his invention. He holds this picture in mind until it has been taken over by the subconscious mind, then relaxes by clearing his mind of ALL thought, and waits for his answer to "flash" into his mind.

Sometimes the results are both definite and immediate. At other times, the results are negative, depending upon the state of development of the "sixth sense," or creative faculty.

Mr. Edison tried out more than 10,000 different combinations of ideas through the synthetic faculty of his imagination before he "tuned in" through the creative faculty, and got the answer which perfected the incandescent light. His experience was similar when he produced the talking machine.

There is plenty of reliable evidence that the faculty of creative imagination exists. This evidence is available through accurate analysis of men who have become leaders in their respective callings, without having had extensive educations. Lincoln was a notable example of a great leader who achieved greatness, through the discovery, and use of his faculty of creative imagination. He discovered, and began to use this faculty as the result of the stimulation of love which he experienced after he met Anne Rutledge, a statement of the highest significance, in connection with the study of the source of genius.

The pages of history are filled with the records of great leaders whose achievements may be traced directly to the influence of women who aroused the creative faculties of their minds, through the stimulation of sex desire. Napoleon Bonaparte was one of these. When inspired by his first wife, Josephine, he was irresistible and invincible. When his "better judgment" or reasoning faculty prompted him to put Josephine aside, he began to decline. His defeat and St. Helena were not far distant.

If good taste would permit, we might easily mention scores of men, well known to the American people, who climbed to great heights of achievement under the stimulating influence of their wives, only to drop back to destruction AFTER money and power went to their heads, and they put aside the old wife for a new one. Napoleon was not the only man to discover that sex influence, *from the right source,* is more powerful than any substitute of expediency, which may be created by mere reason.

The human mind responds to stimulation!

Among the greatest, and most powerful of these stimuli is the urge of sex. When harnessed and transmuted, this driving force is capable of lifting men into that higher sphere of thought which enables them to master the sources of worry and petty annoyance which beset their pathway on the lower plane.

Unfortunately, only the genii have made the discovery. Others have accepted the experience of sex urge, without discovering one of its major potentialities—a fact which accounts for the great number of "others" as compared to the limited number of genii.

For the purpose of refreshing the memory, in connection with the facts available from the biographies of certain men, we here present the names of a few men of outstanding achievement, each of whom was known to have been of a highly sexed nature.

The genius which was their's, undoubtedly found its source of power in transmuted sex energy:

George Washington	Elbert Hubbard
Napoleon Bonaparte	Elbert H. Gary
William Shakespeare	Oscar Wilde
Abraham Lincoln	Woodrow Wilson
Ralph Waldo Emerson	John H. Patterson
Robert Burns	Andrew Jackson
Thomas Jefferson	Enrico Caruso

Your own knowledge of biography will enable you to add to this list. Find, if you can, a single man, in all history of civilization, who achieved outstanding success in any calling, who was not driven by a well developed sex nature.

If you do not wish to rely upon biographies of men not now living, take inventory of those whom you know to be men of great achievement, and see if you can find one among them who is not highly sexed.

Sex energy is the creative energy of all genii.

There never has been, and never will be a great leader, builder, or artist lacking in this driving force of sex.

Surely no one will misunderstand these statements to mean that ALL who are highly sexed are genii! Man attains to the status of a genius ONLY when, and IF, he stimulates his mind so that it draws upon the forces available, through the creative faculty of the imagination. Chief among the stimuli with which this "stepping up" of the vibrations may be produced is sex energy. The mere *possession* of this energy is not sufficient to produce a genius. The energy must be *transmuted* from desire for physical contact, into some *other* form of desire and action, before it will lift one to the status of a genius.

Far from becoming genii, because of great sex desires, the majority of men *lower* themselves, through misunderstanding and misuse of this great force, to the status of the lower animals.

WHY MEN SELDOM SUCCEED BEFORE FORTY

I discovered, from the analysis of over 25,000 people, that men who succeed in an outstanding way, seldom do so before the age of forty, and more often they do not strike their real pace until they are well beyond the age of fifty. This fact was so astounding that it prompted me to go into the study of its cause most carefully, carrying the investigation over a period of more than twelve years.

This study disclosed the fact that the major reason why the majority of men who succeed do not begin to do so before the age of forty to fifty, is their tendency to DISSIPATE their energies through over indulgence in physical expression of the emotion of sex. The majority of men *never* learn that the urge of sex has other possibilities, which far transcend in importance, that of mere physical expression. The majority of those who make this discovery, do so *after having wasted many years* at a period when the sex energy is at its height, prior to the age of forty-five to fifty. This usually is followed by noteworthy achievement.

The lives of many men up to, and sometimes well past the age of forty, reflect a continued dissipation of energies, which could have been more profitably turned into better channels. Their finer and more powerful emotions are sown wildly to the four winds. Out of this habit of the male, grew the term, "sowing his wild oats."

The desire for sexual expression is by far the strongest and most impelling of all the human emotions, and for this very reason this desire, when *harnessed and transmuted* into action, other than that of physical expression, may raise one to the status of a genius.

One of America's most able business men frankly admitted that his attractive secretary was responsible for most of the plans he created. He admitted that her presence lifted him to heights of creative imagination, such as he could experience under no other stimulus.

One of the most successful men in America owes most of his success to the influence of a very charming young woman, who has served as his source of inspiration for more than twelve years. Everyone knows the man to whom this reference is made, but not everyone knows the REAL SOURCE of his achievements.

History is not lacking in examples of men who attained to the status of genii, as the result of the use of artificial mind stimulants in the form of alcohol and narcotics. Edgar Allen Poe wrote the "Raven" while under the influence of liquor, "dreaming dreams that mortal never dared to dream before." James Whitcomb Riley did his best writing while under the influence of alcohol. Perhaps it was thus he saw "the ordered intermingling of the real and the dream, the mill above the river, and the mist above the stream." Robert Burns wrote best when intoxicated, "For Auld Lang Syne, my dear, we'll take a cup of kindness yet, for Auld Lang Syne."

But let it be remembered that many such men have destroyed themselves in the end. Nature has prepared her own potions with which men may safely stimulate their minds so they vibrate on a plane that enables them to tune in to fine and rare thoughts which come from—no man knows where! No satisfactory substitute for Nature's stimulants has ever been found.

It is a fact well known to psychologists that there is a very close relationship between sex desires and spiritual urges—a fact which accounts for the peculiar behavior of people who participate in the orgies known as religious "revivals," common among the primitive types.

The world is ruled, and the destiny of civilization is established, by the human emotions. People are influenced in their actions, not by reason so much as by "feelings." The creative faculty of the mind is set into action entirely by emotions, and *not by cold reason.* The most powerful of all human emotions is that of sex. There are other mind stimulants, some of which have been listed, but no one of them, nor all of them combined, can equal the driving power of sex.

A mind stimulant is any influence which will either temporarily, or permanently, increase the vibrations of thought. The ten major stimulants, described, are those most commonly resorted to. Through these sources one may commune with Infinite Intelligence, or enter, at will, the store-house of the subconscious mind, either one's own, or that of another person, a procedure *which is all there is of genius.*

A teacher, who has trained and directed the efforts of more than 30,000 sales people, made the astounding discovery that highly sexed men are the most efficient salesmen. The explanation is, that the factor of personality known as "personal magnetism" is nothing more nor less than sex energy. Highly sexed people always have a plentiful supply of magnetism. Through cultivation and understanding, this vital force may be drawn upon and used to great advantage in the relationships between people. This energy may be communicated to others through the following media:

1. The hand-shake. The touch of the hand indicates, instantly, the presence of magnetism, or the lack of it.

2. The tone of voice. Magnetism, or sex energy, is the factor with which the voice may be colored, or made musical and charming.

3. Posture and carriage of the body. Highly sexed people move briskly, and with grace and ease.

4. The vibrations of thought. Highly sexed people mix the emotion of sex with their thoughts, or may do so at will, and in that way, may influence those around them.

5. Body adornment. People who are highly sexed are usually very careful about their personal appearance. They usually select clothing of a style becoming to their personality, physique, complexion, etc.

When employing salesmen, the more capable sales manager looks for the quality of personal magnetism as the *first requirement* of a salesman.

People who lack sex energy will never become enthusiastic nor inspire others with enthusiasm, and enthusiasm is one of the most important requisites in salesmanship, no matter what one is selling.

The public speaker, orator, preacher, lawyer, or salesman who is lacking in sex energy is a "flop," as far as being able to influence others is concerned. Couple with this the fact, that most people can be influenced only through an appeal to their emotions, and you will understand the importance of sex energy as a part of the salesman's native ability. Master salesmen attain the status of mastery in selling, because they, either consciously, or unconsciously, *transmute* the energy of sex into SALES ENTHUSIASM! In this statement may be found a very practical suggestion as to the actual meaning of sex transmutation.

The salesman who knows how to take his mind off the subject of sex, and direct it in sales effort with as much enthusiasm and determination as he would apply to its original purpose, has acquired the art of sex transmutation, whether he knows it or not. The majority of salesmen who transmute their sex energy do so without being in the least aware of what they are doing, or how they are doing it.

Transmutation of sex energy calls for more will power than the average person cares to use for this purpose. Those who find it difficult to summon will-power sufficient for transmutation, may gradually acquire this ability. Though this requires will-power, the reward for the practice is more than worth the effort.

The entire subject of sex is one with which the majority of people appear to be unpardonably ignorant. The urge of sex has been grossly misunderstood, slandered, and burlesqued by the ignorant and the evil minded, for so long that the very word sex is seldom used in polite society. Men and women who are known to be blessed—yes, BLESSED—with highly sexed natures, are usually looked upon as being people who will bear watching. Instead of being called blessed, they are usually called cursed.

Millions of people, even in this age of enlightenment, have inferiority complexes which they developed because of this false belief that a highly sexed nature is a curse. These statements, of the virtue of sex energy, should not be construed as justification for the libertine. The emotion of sex is a virtue ONLY when used intelligently, and with discrimination. It may be misused, and often is, to such an extent that it debases, instead of enriches, both body and mind. The better use of this power is the burden of this chapter.

It seemed quite significant to the author, when he made the discovery that practically every great leader, whom he had the privilege of analyzing, was a man whose achievements were largely inspired by a woman. In many instances, the "woman in the case" was a modest, self-denying wife, of whom the public had heard but little or nothing. In a few instances, the source of inspiration has been traced to the "other woman." Perhaps such cases may not be entirely unknown to you.

Intemperance in sex habits is just as detrimental as intemperance in habits of drinking and eating. In this age in which we live, an age which began with the world war, intemperance in habits of sex is common. This orgy of indulgence may account for the shortage of great leaders. No man can avail himself of the forces of his creative imagination, while dissipating them. Man is the only creature on earth which violates Nature's purpose in this connection. Every other animal indulges its sex nature in moderation, and with purpose which harmonizes with the laws of nature. Every other animal responds to the call of sex only in "season." Man's inclination is to declare "open season."

Every intelligent person knows that stimulation in excess, through alcoholic drink and narcotics, is a form of intemperance which destroys the vital organs of the body, including the brain. Not every person knows, however, that over indulgence in sex expression may become a habit as destructive and as detrimental to creative effort as narcotics or liquor.

A sex-mad man is not essentially different than a dope-mad man! Both have lost control over their faculties of reason and will-power. Sexual overindulgence may not only destroy reason and willpower, but it may also lead to either temporary, or permanent insanity. Many cases of hypochondria (imaginary illness) grow out of habits developed in ignorance of the true function of sex.

From these brief references to the subject, it may be readily seen that ignorance on the subject of sex transmutation, forces stupendous penalties upon the ignorant on the one hand, and withholds from them equally stupendous benefits, on the other.

Widespread ignorance on the subject of sex is due to the fact that the subject has been surrounded with mystery and beclouded by dark silence. The conspiracy of mystery and silence has had the same effect upon the minds of young people that the psychology of prohibition had. The result has been increased curiosity, and desire to acquire more knowledge on this "verboten" subject; and to the shame of all lawmakers, and most physicians— by training best qualified to educate youth on that subject—information has not been easily available.

Seldom does an individual enter upon highly creative effort in any field of endeavor before the age of forty. The average man reaches the period of his greatest capacity to create between forty and sixty.

These statements are based upon analysis of thousands of men and women who have been carefully observed. They should be encouraging to those who fail to arrive before the age of forty, and to those who become frightened at the approach of "old age," around the forty-year mark. The years between forty and fifty are, as a rule, the most fruitful. Man should approach this age, not with fear and trembling, but with hope and eager anticipation.

If you want evidence that most men do not begin to do their best work before the age of forty, study the records of the most successful men known to the American people, and you will find it. Henry Ford had not "hit his pace" of achievement until he had passed the age of forty. Andrew Carnegie was well past forty before he began to reap the reward of his efforts. James J. Hill was still running a telegraph key at the age of forty. His stupendous achievements took place after that age. Biographies of American industrialists and financiers are filled with evidence that the period from forty to sixty is the most productive age of man.

Between the ages of thirty and forty, man begins to learn (if he ever learns), the art of sex transmutation. This discovery is generally accidental, and more often than otherwise, the man who makes it is totally unconscious of his discovery. He may observe that his powers of achievement have increased around the age of thirty-five to forty, but in most cases, he is not familiar with the cause of this change; that Nature begins to harmonize the emotions of love and sex in the individual, between the ages of thirty and forty, so that he may draw upon these great forces, and apply them jointly as stimuli to action.

Sex, alone, is a mighty urge to action, but its forces are like a cyclone—they are often uncontrollable. When the emotion of love begins to mix itself with the emotion of sex, the result is calmness of purpose, poise, accuracy of judgment, and balance. What person, who has attained to the age of forty, is so unfortunate as to be unable to analyze these statements, and to corroborate them by his own experience?

When driven by his desire to please a woman, based solely upon the emotion of sex, a man may be, and usually is, capable of great achievement, but his actions may be disorganized, distorted, and totally destructive. When driven by his desire to please a woman, based upon the motive of sex alone, a man may steal, cheat, and even commit murder. But when the emotion of LOVE is mixed with the emotion of sex, that same man will guide his actions with more sanity, balance, and reason.

Criminologists have discovered that the most hardened criminals can be reformed through the influence of a woman's *love*. There is no record of a criminal having been reformed solely through the sex influence. These facts are well known, but their cause is not. Reformation comes, if at all, through the *heart*, or the emotional side of man, *not* through his head, or reasoning side. Reformation means, "a change of heart." It does not mean a "change of head." A man may, because of reason, make certain changes in his personal conduct to avoid the consequences of undesirable effects, but GENUINE REFORMATION comes only through a change of heart—through a DESIRE to change.

Love, Romance, and Sex are all emotions capable of driving men to heights of super achievement. Love is the emotion which serves as a safety valve, and insures balance, poise, and constructive effort. When combined, these three emotions may lift one to an altitude of a genius. There are genii, however, who know but little of the emotion of love. Most of them may be found engaged in some form of action which is destructive, or at least, not based upon justice and fairness toward others. If good taste would permit, a dozen genii could be named in the field of industry and finance, who ride ruthlessly over the rights of their fellow men. They seem totally lacking in conscience. The reader can easily supply his own list of such men.

The emotions are states of mind. Nature has provided man with a "chemistry of the mind" which operates in a manner similar to the principles of chemistry of matter. It is a well known fact that, through the aid of chemistry of matter, a chemist may create a deadly poison by mixing certain elements, none of which are—in themselves—harmful in the right proportions. The emotions may, likewise, be combined so as to create a deadly poison. The emotions of sex and jealousy, when mixed, may turn a person into an insane beast.

The presence of any one or more of the destructive emotions in the human mind, through the chemistry of the mind, sets up a poison which may destroy one's sense of justice and fairness. In extreme cases, the presence of any combination of these emotions in the mind may destroy one's reason.

The road to genius consists of the development, control, and use of sex, love, and romance. Briefly, the process may be stated as follows:

Encourage the presence of these emotions as the dominating thoughts in one's mind, and discourage the presence of all the destructive emotions. The mind is a creature of habit. It thrives upon the *dominating* thoughts fed it. Through the faculty of will-power, one may discourage the presence of any emotion, and encourage the presence of any other. Control of the mind, through the power of will, is not difficult. Control comes from persistence, and habit. The secret of control lies in understanding the process of transmutation. When any negative emotion presents itself in one's mind, it can be transmuted into a positive, or constructive emotion, by the simple procedure of changing one's thoughts.

THERE IS NO OTHER ROAD TO GENIUS THAN THROUGH VOLUNTARY SELF EFFORT! A man may attain to great heights of financial or business achievement, solely by the driving force of sex energy, but history is filled with evidence that he may, and usually does, carry with him certain traits of character which rob him of the ability to either hold, or enjoy his fortune. This is worthy of analysis, thought, and meditation, for it states a truth, the knowledge of which may be helpful to women as well as men. Ignorance of this has cost thousands of people their privilege of HAPPINESS, even though they possessed riches.

The emotions of love and sex leave their unmistakable marks upon the features. Moreover, these signs are so visible, that all who wish may read them. The man who is driven by the storm of passion, based upon sex desires alone, plainly advertises that fact to the entire world, by the expression of his eyes, and the lines of his face. The emotion of love, when mixed with the emotion of sex, softens, modifies, and beautifies the facial expression. No character analyst is needed to tell you this—you may observe it for yourself.

The emotion of love brings out, and develops, the artistic and the aesthetic nature of man. It leaves its impress upon one's very soul, even after the fire has been subdued by time and circumstance.

Memories of love never pass. They linger, guide, and influence long after the source of stimulation has faded. There is nothing new in this. Every person, who has been moved by GENUINE LOVE, knows that it leaves enduring traces upon the human heart. The effect of love endures, because love is spiritual in nature. The man who cannot be stimulated to great heights of achievement by love, is hopeless—he is dead, though he may seem to live.

Even the memories of love are sufficient to lift one to a higher plane of creative effort. The major force of love may spend itself and pass away, like a fire which has burned itself out, but it leaves behind indelible marks as evidence that it passed that way. Its departure often prepares the human heart for a still greater love.

Go back into your yesterdays, at times, and bathe your mind in the beautiful memories of past love. It will soften the influence of the present worries and annoyances. It will give you a source of escape from the unpleasant realities of life, and maybe—who knows?—your mind will yield to you, during this temporary retreat into the world of fantasy, ideas, or plans which may change the entire financial or spiritual status of your life.

If you believe yourself unfortunate, because you have "loved and lost," perish the thought. One who has loved truly, can never lose entirely. Love is whimsical and temperamental. Its nature is ephemeral, and transitory. It comes when it pleases, and goes away without warning. Accept and enjoy it while it remains, but spend no time worrying about its departure. Worry will never bring it back.

Dismiss, also, the thought that love never comes but once. Love may come and go, times without number, but there are no two love experiences which affect one in just the same way. There may be, and there usually is, one love experience which leaves a deeper imprint on the heart than all the others, but all love experiences are beneficial, except to the person who becomes resentful and cynical when love makes its departure.

There should be no disappointment over love, and there would be none if people understood the difference between the emotions of love and sex. The major difference is that love is spiritual, while sex is biological. No experience, which touches the human heart with a spiritual force, can possibly be harmful, except through ignorance, or jealousy.

Love is, without question, life's greatest experience. It brings one into communion with Infinite Intelligence. When mixed with the emotions of romance and sex, it may lead one far up the ladder of creative effort. The emotions of love, sex, and romance, are sides of the eternal triangle of achievement-building genius. Nature creates genii through no other force.

Love is an emotion with many sides, shades, and colors. The love which one feels for parents, or children is quite different from that which one feels for one's sweetheart. The one is mixed with the emotion of sex, while the other is not.

The love which one feels in true friendship is not the same as that felt for one's sweetheart, parents, or children, but it, too, is a form of love.

Then, there is the emotion of love for things inanimate, such as the love of Nature's handiwork. But the most intense and burning of all these various kinds of love, is that experienced in the blending of the emotions of love and sex. Marriages, not blessed with the eternal affinity of love, properly balanced and proportioned, with sex, cannot be happy ones— and seldom endure. Love, alone, will not bring happiness in marriage, nor will sex alone. When these two beautiful emotions are blended, marriage may bring about a state of mind, closest to the spiritual that one may ever know on this earthly plane.

When the emotion of romance is added to those of love and sex, the obstructions between the finite mind of man and Infinite Intelligence are removed. Then a genius has been born!

What a different story is this, than those usually associated with the emotion of sex. Here is an interpretation of the emotion which lifts it out of the commonplace, and makes of it potter's clay in the hands of God, from which He fashions all that is beautiful and inspiring. It is an interpretation which would, when properly understood, bring harmony out of the chaos which exists in too many marriages. The disharmonies often expressed in the form of nagging, may usually be traced to *lack of knowledge* on the subject of sex. Where love, romance and the proper understanding of the emotion and function of sex abide, there is no disharmony between married people.

Fortunate is the husband whose wife understands the true relationship between the emotions of love, sex, and romance. When motivated by this holy triumvirate, no form of labor is burdensome, because even the most lowly form of effort takes on the nature of a labor of love.

It is a very old saying that "a man's wife may either make him or break him," but the reason is not always understood. The "making" and "breaking" is the result of the wife's understanding, or lack of understanding of the emotions of love, sex, and romance.

Despite the fact that men are polygamous, by the very nature of their biological inheritance, it is true that no woman has as great an influence on a man as his wife, unless he is married to a woman totally unsuited to his nature. If a woman permits her husband to lose interest in her, and become more interested in other women, it is usually because of her ignorance, or indifference toward the subjects of sex, love, and romance. This statement presupposes, of course, that genuine love once existed between a man and his wife. The facts are equally applicable to a man who permits his wife's interest in him to die.

Married people often bicker over a multitude of trivialities. If these are analyzed accurately, the real cause of the trouble will often be found to be indifference, or ignorance on these subjects.

Man's greatest motivating force is his desire to please woman! The hunter who excelled during prehistoric days, before the dawn of civilization, did so, because of his desire to appear great in the eyes of woman. Man's nature has not changed in this respect. The "hunter" of today brings home no skins of wild animals, but he indicates his desire for her favor by supplying fine clothes, motor cars, and wealth. Man has the same desire to please woman that he had before the dawn of civilization. The only thing that has changed, is his method of pleasing. Men who accumulate large fortunes, and attain to great heights of power and fame, do so, mainly, to satisfy their *desire to please women*. Take women out of their lives, and great wealth would be useless to most men. *It is this inherent desire of man to please woman, which gives woman the power to make or break a man.*

The woman who understands man's nature and tactfully caters to it, need have no fear of competition from other women. Men may be "giants" with indomitable will-power when dealing with other men, but they are easily managed by the women of their choice.

Most men will not admit that they are easily influenced by the women they prefer, because it is in the nature of the male to want to be recognized as the stronger of the species. Moreover, the intelligent woman recognizes this "manly trait" and very wisely makes no issue of it.

Some men know that they are being influenced by the women of their choice—their wives, sweethearts, mothers or sisters—but they tactfully refrain from rebelling against the influence because they are intelligent enough to know that NO MAN IS HAPPY OR COMPLETE WITHOUT THE MODIFYING INFLUENCE OF THE RIGHT WOMAN. The man who does not recognize this important truth deprives himself of the power which has done more to help men achieve success than all other forces combined.

9 781722 502652